A MESSAGE FOR YOU

AKILA MUKARRAMMA

Copyright © 2013 by Akila Mukarramma

Published by:
Voices Books & Publishing
P.O. Box 3007
Bridgeton, MO 63044
www.voicesbooks.homestead.com

Printed in the United States of America

All rights reserved. No part of this publication may be reproduced, stored in a retrieval system, or transmitted in any form or by any means, electronic, mechanical, recording or otherwise, without the prior written permission of the author.

Library of Congress Catalog Card No.: On File

ISBN: 978-1492325581

A Message for You

A message is vital information given that we may benefit and govern ourselves accordingly. Not all messages are verbal. Messages are many forms; things we hear as well as see. If we stay focused by keeping things real and simple, we will be able to recognize and receive our messages.

Height & Gravity

The more we expand our mind in thought and imagination, the more we learn of ourselves. We are a people created from a source that masters all properties of change, which is time.
Information is the source of our being

The heart is the soul of spirit, which is truth and truth governs the compass of our heart. The mind is a vault of information and memories that aid in making our decisions from our past to our present.

When we are looking for solutions to our problems, we are burden with many thoughts, trying to make sense out of confusion. We being spiritual, mystical creatures without weight or sound, travel through time without gravity. Gravity is the force of weight that grounds matter.

Anything the mind can imagine and vision is nothing more than the memory of time. This is why concentration and meditation is important that we may relax and let the answers unfold. When we do this, our burdens no longer weigh us down and we are able to excel and listen.

A Message Over Heard

One fine, sunny day as I was walking to the bus stop on my way to work, I heard a woman say to another woman "Hang in there." Immediately I felt the vibration of that message in my soul. As I continued to walk to the bus stop, I could not stop thinking about those words, "Hang in there." Why did I have to hear that phrase of all things? As if, I did not have enough to worry about in my life.

I was a letter sorter at the Post Office and was able to sit as I cased my mail, which gave me a lot of time to think. Why, what and who was coming my way? The suspense was killing me. After two hours of working, it was time for my break. I went to the break area and kicked it with my co-workers and still nothing out of the ordinary. As I proceeded to walk back to my workstation, the attendance supervisor approached me and said, "Your family is fine, your sister is on her way to get you and your house is on fire."

"Damn, there it is, "Hang in there," I knew that message was for me. The mystery was over. I thanked the Creator for giving me notice to be alert for the unexpected. I was grateful and thankful that my children were safe and that I would not have to delay any time getting to them. Anything after that was material.

A warning sign went out to prepare me for my endeavor and my many thanks to my supervisor, for her thoughtfulness and compassion the way she delivered that message to me.

What is your message for the day?
Turn the pages and see.

The Complexion of Change

When we make the right decisions, our lifestyles change for the better. We replace old ideas with new ideas and old thoughts with new thoughts.

We realize that responsibility is vital to our growth and life is the awareness of self. The lessons we learn in life, teach us that consciousness is the power to make changes. Once we make the necessary changes in our lives, we have just removed the obstacles out of our paths.

Now is that not a beautiful complexion of character?

Imitation Flavor

We must be careful how we choose our paths
many times
we make decisions
that
result
in
more consequences
than
rewards

We make excuses when we are careless with our choices
We must realize
that
our choices have contracts
and
our decision binds us to them

If
we want the authentic flavor of life
then
we must stay true to ourselves
and
seek for the real flavor of life
and
not an imitation

Pray for Yourself

Who can pray for you better than you can pray for yourself?

Who knows your circumstances better than you?

This
is
your cry for help
Once
you have done
all
you can do
know
that
prayer is the strength of enduring patience
&
like bread
you
must let it rise

Circumstances play a devastating role in our lives. We become frustrated and impatient for change, allowing anxiety to rule rather than common sense. Anxiety causes us to make irrational decisions, which only make matters worse. If we would only rest in truth, which is time, we will be able to see our prayers unfold.

To Help Someone Else is to Help yourself

Thoughtfulness
returns in ways unimaginable
our
lives
become enhanced
and
our paths, are made simple

The gratification of making a difference in someone else's life is phenomenal. We live not in this world alone and we need each other. We never know when our hour of need will arrive; therefore, let us keep an open heart to give back the gift of love.

A grain of Truth is Nourishment to the Soul

If
we are honest
with
ourselves
and
address our negatives
as
well as our positives
we
heal

Truth is the reality of time because, it happened. Although, many have tried to change truth with convincing lies, know that truth is the manifestation of time.

Our Conscience is our Guide

The
breath that sustains life
is
the breath
that
gives us thought and imagination
When we are at the point of giving up, we need to pause.
Take a deep breath and summon the highest form of
thought the imagination of change.

Many times in our struggles, we need rejuvenation because, the challenges and disappointments we encounter, drain us to the point of humiliation & defeat. Know that the small voice in our mind that never ceases to correct us when we are debatable within ourselves is our conscience relaying information of truth. Information is the light that over sees our footsteps.

The
more we think we know
the
more we realize
we
do not know
learn
to
trust
the quiet voice within
and
ask for guidance
from
the
giver
of
truth & imagination

Love is Respect & Respect is Love

When
we display common courtesy, we demonstrate
love
the
greatest reward is to retire in the eve of the day
knowing
you gave the best of yourself
by
demonstrating your measures of understanding
on
the highest level

Now
someone knows the meaning of love
because
you gave them respect

Silence has Never gone to Court for Slander

Sometimes in life
it is
better to hold your tongue
rather
than to speak

Fret not

Time & Truth
keeps
memory of all things

When speaking on the affairs of others
remember
to
keep self in mind
because
the
file on self
has
more than enough information
to
sink a boat
or
bury you for life

Therefore
learn to speak
with
discretion & understanding

We
need not try to discredit others
to
try & make ourselves look good

The
time & energy
we
spend with our opinions
about
someone else's life
needs
to
be applied to analyzing
our
own faults & mistakes

Assumption & Accusation

Are
all the facts present

Many
people have suffered
by
the tongue of assumption & accusation

Assumption is inadequate information and accusation is not a proven fact. Our pre-conceived minds have destroyed many lives, livelihoods and relationships with false information.

Know that errors of the tongue is pollution in the air
be
conscious of the information
you
release on others
because
you, could very well be the next victim

The Biggest Dare in Life is to Challenge Yourself

One of man's greatest fears
is
to fail

Not
realizing
failing is a part of achieving

Understand
you cannot learn to walk without the trauma of falling. We stumble only to regain balance when certain experiences overwhelm us.
We
must pause
&
re-think our choices to gather ourselves

As
we look back over our lives
&
see the obstacles we have overcome
we
realize
our
past
is
our
teacher, text & history

The lessons we encounter are priceless and they teach us to believe in ourselves. Every time we challenge self by giving our best, we master our weaknesses and overcome our fears. We become proud and feel stronger within ourselves, ready to tackle and conquer the next battle between our strengths and weakness.

Stress and Depression

We panic when we do not see the solution.
Not realizing that every problem has a solution and there is nothing new under the sun that truth cannot heal. There is no positive without negative or negative without positive; they both are one.

We are composed with the same negative and positive
energy
to
maintain balance and stability.

When we face circumstances that are out of our control, we become irritated and disturbed. Adversity is the result of bad choices and we become prisoners in our own decisions. Who can free the mind of despair when it is plagued with fear and doubt? Nothing seems to satisfy the soul and we become an enemy within ourselves.

Depression is a negative state of mind that wrestles with the positive to keep the mind confused. Our challenges will make us stronger if we are patient within ourselves and know that everything grows, change & heal with time.

Friends Cannot Be Weighed Against Dollars & Cents

Wisdom has taught us that the borrower becomes slave to the lender. Value your friendship and return the gift in the same manner in which you received it, from me to you.

Trust is the link that binds us together and we must protect it by giving the same compassion of respect

given

to

us

at the time

of

our request

that

our friendship continues

to

hold validity

Wisdom's Thoughts

On
a creative note
where much is inspired
to
a preferred taste
where
much is desired
Left or Right
is
it good, is it bad
constructive criticism, one more, should I add
should
I
stay
should
I
go

Answer yes answer no
to
build up or tear down
THOUGHTS
What is best for now?

Let
not your emotions
over rule
and
tip the scale
of
good judgment

Let us strengthen our constitution of dignity & integrity
understanding
is
the black robe
that
gives
justice to the meek & humble

Opportunity
is
ours
to
make
a
wrong right

Painful Memories

Often time
we
are
visited
with
certain memories of our forgotten past
to
remind us of our victories
that
we may overcome
our
present struggles

Yesterday, gave us victory for today
life is a cycle that repeats itself through time. In the mist
of
change, we encounter many challenges and
disappointments. Some so strenuous that we feel as
though life has no purpose.

We cringe at the thought of circumstances and situations
of yesterday because they were so painful. Then we
realized we made it through those horrible times and the
memories are only to make us stronger.

Patience is Listening & Thinking

Sometimes
we find ourselves
stopped
in
our tracks
limited in situations
and
rejected or ejected
for
no apparent reason

We
are being summoned
to
listen
to
our thoughts
to
Evaluate & Revise
them

Truth Changes for No One
Ask
The Bleeding Heart

Many times
we are faced with truths
we
are
not ready to accept

Nevertheless
it
is
a
truth

Rather than lose direction & stability, let us think with
logic and reasoning. Life is for the mind to experiment &
explore. Truth is the evidence of time. Therefore
live your life through the eye of wisdom
&
find
your
place in the Sun

One day, as I was smiling
I
was thinking

Today, I did the right thing
&
made someone else happy besides myself

We, have always been told that it is better to give
than it is to receive

Now I understand the measure of a gift

Oh Love, Catch Me

Please
do not let me
fall
For, in my hour
of
deep distress
please
hasten to answer
my call
so
many I see
with
bow down heads
so
many are numb
from
the tears they have shed
My
heart is humble
my
tongue is still
Instead
Of
passing judgment

I pray, for love to heal

An Open Mind is the Scholar of Time

It
is
only
when our minds are open
to
understand

That
we are no longer
afraid
to
let
reason
counsel & quiet us
that
our fears may cease
with
knowledge and understanding

Make no mistake
we
should
always be able to smell our own stink
before
we go sniffing out someone else's unpleasant odors
None of us is perfect
We
all have secrets & ill thoughts
There
comes a time in life when we need
a
Soul & Mirror check confession
to
admit
to
our ugly ways
that
we make not the mistake of thinking
we
are
beyond error

Are
thoughts & ideas of one's understanding
expressed
among those who share breath

Regardless
of
language, culture or race
truth
is
the presence of time

We all have an opinion and sometimes we become emotional in our expression of explanation and the discussion becomes emotional and confrontational. Remember, everyone listens and learns differently, according to the way he or she, understands. Once we realize that we have different expressions of explanation, we will be able to communicate respectfully with one another.
Because
we
all understand laughter & tears.

Soul Satisfied

Just as the sun
passes through the day
so
is
the newness of a gift that is fashioned by hands
only
treasures of the heart
can
satisfy the soul

One
is
never truly happy
until
the soul is satisfied

Material gain accommodates the physical needs. The soul
desires a peace of mind.

Love is waking up with the one on your mind

rather

than to just have one in your bed

Too many people wake up and say good morning to strangers
two bodies
fishing for words of dedication
chemistry is the plank that balances between two hearts.

Take note, it is the fire that burns in the soul that keeps the bed warm.

A Reason to Live

Life
is
reasoning
within
itself

Think!
Who can argue with time?

Rise and make each day a beautiful memory
of
yesterday, discovering self
by
giving life all you have to give

A Deaf Ear

Listening
is
hard
when you have
your
own
agenda

When we have our minds made up
and
stubborn to the fact of listening to reason
we
cripple ourselves and make time-consuming mistakes

Minding Your Own Business

Everybody's business is not your business

By
the same token
your
business
is
not
everybody's

Take a moment
to
think!

Everyone has a right to privacy and space
Someone
else's business cannot add one
"Iota"
to
your life
&
by the same token,
your
business
cannot add one "iota" to theirs

Helplessness, is without reason

A weakness, we tell ourselves is a sickness and we are void of control!
Our actions & habits are self-indulgence, which causes us to suffer the consequences or re-action for an action

Deep in our heart, a voice is saying, abuse. If you love yourself, truth makes you realize that you have become a victim of your own bad choices.

This is when you stop and say, "Enough is enough"! It is time to take responsibility for my actions. We are in control and our reason is the only thing that will support our decision. Either, we can be for real with ourselves or terribly deny our common sense to save us from self-destruction. The choice of decision is all we have to stand on for positive results.
"Pocket Change for Life" stated, "Reason is discipline."

Helplessness' is without reason

3 Packs A Day

I use to smoke three packs of cigarettes a day. When it came time for me to quit, I first asked my higher power, (the one who created me) to help me help myself because, this is where I draw my strength. Like a parent to a child, to assist me. I put myself into a spiritual realm, depending on nothing but my reason. My reason was just that, my reason. Ask yourself, how many things do you do out of reason?
I will share my reasons with you. I told the urge to smoke that although the cigarette was good that I no longer cared to indulge myself. I did not run from the craving instead, I spoke my reason out verbally that I may hear the truth I was standing on. I would say, "I want you but I don't need you because, you gave me chest pains and the nicotine has engulfed my body."

As I attempted my quest, a man came to me and told me that if I could make it seventy -two hours, (three days) without a cigarette that I had it made. I said, "Bet" because I was ready and real with myself and kept my reason before me. I wanted to be free of the discomfort I was feeling with those cigarettes. We do live with choice and decision. Every time someone would light up, I would not run, rather, I faced my weakness with my reason until I no longer craved for the poison that was killing me.

I was successful because, my reason became a part of me and it took over and became my strength. I kept reminding myself the reason why I chose to no longer smoke. Now when I smell a cigarette it chokes me because, my lungs have cleared up.

Now, think to yourself and find a reason for your (discipline). Concentrate on the reward and no longer be a prisoner of the consequence and prove to yourself you can do anything you put your mind too. After all, our concept of living is choice and decision. Stand on your Reason.

MOTIVATE the SOUL WITH understanding

Let us heal
our
thoughts
by
seeking our desires

We cannot reverse time or change yesterday
only
draw strengths from the lesson we learned

Take note
Yesterday had its reasons for its pain & disappointments

Today with growth
we
now understand

Procrastination

Is
time ignored

The elders always told us not to put things off we can do
today

Every time we awake
it's
today

You Cannot House the Creator

However, many try
with
Oaths and Creeds

Only

to
forget
more than they remember

Justice
teaches
us
to
just
be
real with ourselves

And

the
world will know & remember you
as
one of trust

Be Effective

When you make
a
difference
in
someone's life

A
difference
can
be
made in yours

Learn
to give of yourself
that
life may give back to you

Maturity

Life
is
to
learn self
that
our choices
may
reward us

Growing
from
childhood to adulthood
is
the
most crucial time for bad choices
living out of our fantasies
and
not realizing the consequences

Finally
we learn to take responsibility
for
our actions
because
now
we have lived enough
to
understand
the wisdom of time

Connection

When we reach out
to
others
we
meet our Spiritual
Family

Although we may share a womb
and
a mother's breast
our
walk in life
leads us to meet and bond
with
our spiritual connections
which
last forever

A Child is a Growing Mind

Therefore
as
an
adult
let us entertain
the
thought of explanation

That
our children may grow
with
balance and understanding

To Seek is to Find & Master Self

Many of us spend half a lifetime
looking
for
someone to save us
until
we realize
our
hero is the truth within

Life is a Conversation without Pause

Each day gives us something
to
talk about

With
Common Interest

Simplicity is the Balance of Life

We
make simple things
complicated
when
we try to replace
fact with fiction

Listening
Is
The Student Within

We
learn by listening
and
paying attention

Regardless
of
yesterday's blueprint
we
come to realize
that
everyday is an education within itself

SEX

The ultimate pleasure
of
life
became
a
lustful fantasy
without
purpose

Sex
has been placed
in
the
category of sin
making
whores out of women
and
women out of men

Finding our Strengths is Overcoming our Weaknesses

Labor
with your insecurities
and
challenge yourself
to
the fullest
that
you may realize the power within

SELFISHNESS

Is
the lack
of
understanding

Someone held you when you took your first breath
Someone fed you to keep you from starving to death
There has always been a lamp at the core of our feet
to pave the way for you and me

Selfishness is the inability to recognize
you
are not
alone

FREEDOM

Is
mental as well as physical

When you are the first to realize your mistakes, you are free.
Freedom
allows you to laugh at yourself
because
imperfection is nothing to hide.

The beauty of being free to laugh at yourself is your accreditation of honesty. People are more incline to trust someone who accepts their own realities of imperfection than one who pretends perfection. This characteristic lays the foundation for a perfect relationship among humanity.

COMMUNICATION

Communication is reasoning with Understanding

Understanding is the mediator of peace
we
learn from many aspects of life

Information
is
exchangeable
therefore
communication
is
the space between
two lines
or
the
positive and the negative
that
balances
more
than one opinion

Slavery

Slavery stops the thought process
and
makes one dependent

When
a person stops thinking for himself
and
makes his own decisions
he
becomes
incompetent

Your
mind is your navigator to freedom

Keep it open
and
exercise your thoughts
that
you are able to stand
accountable

Life is About Change

Everyday is full of choices, challenges and decisions.
Sometimes we find ourselves in a comfort zone
and
hesitate not to move when time is calling for change.
The fear of not knowing what to expect, overwhelms us
when
we cannot see into the unknown.

But
if we look back into our library of memories
&
count our victories of yesterday
as
we entertain Truth
we
feel safe
because
life is about change

A Strong Woman needs a Strong Man

Some men and women require more than others do
and
some endure more than others do

How
can one support the other
if
understanding
is
not
the foundation of a relationship?

Treasures of the Heart

The ugliest part on my body was the first thing you said, you loved about me. After the shadow of pain & disappointment, I was afraid to trust the compassion of love so I ran. Hoping you would catch me and then I would know, you cared and I was yours forever.

You captured me & suddenly I realized that my running away was over. I could no longer hide my feelings. You were the one for me and I was the one for you. Like a magnet, I think about you and you appear. You reach for me and I am in your arms before my next breath. All I can do is surrender.

You stripped me of all my secrets and I now stand naked before you, trying to hold back my tears. Overwhelmed, I have no choice but to confess, my love for you as we sink deep into the passion of imagination. Come let us explore the gift of time, which is forever.

The message
of
true love is the reality within
We
have no need to pretend

There are no scripts
just
You & Me

Low Self Esteem

Comes from disappointment within one's self

There are times, in our challenges we feel defeated and do not know how to retrieve our confidence. We feel as though the loss of energy is irretrievable & there is no purpose or reason for today
We all have fears that haunt us but life is our fascinating story and we all have one to tell
perfection cannot be the star
because
there would be no ups and downs
no
disappointments and tears
only
perfection and heroic lies
which
no one wants to hear
because
there would be nothing to gain

Therefore

be not
a
victim
of
low self-esteem

TRUE LOVE

Is
having respect for truth

MATH

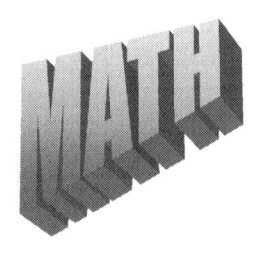

Every problem has a solution

How else
can there be a complete circle?
A
circle ends, where it begins

Life
!

Yesterday's questions are today's answers

BUSY BODIES

Are
people with misdirected energy
They are unable to see and correct their own mistakes
because
they are busy meddling in other folks business

A
word of wisdom

If
you cannot help or heal
let
time and truth handle its business
&
you handle yours

ROCK SCHOOL

You
must pay attention to win
the rock, is transferred behind the back
From
Hand to Hand
you
sit on the steps
&
when the hands become visible
you
must guess the hand the rock is in

If
you choose correctly
you
elevate, to the next step (level)
until
there are no more steps then you become the teacher

A Process in life

Laws

There are laws of the land
&
the laws of man

The
laws of the land prevail
while
the laws of man
crumble
with
lies and deceit

The Spirit of a Person

Is
deeper than the color of one's skin

The color of one's skin is the result of ones origin
geography
&
circumstances separate us for various reasons
we
cripple ourselves
when
we let ignorance rule
&
refuse
to
open our eyes
to
the
truths
of
life

A CRUTCH

Props support us when we are unable to stabilize ourselves. When we become dependent, we no longer depend on our strengths. We deny ourselves the greatest experience of accomplishments

We can accomplish anything with determination & understanding

TOMORROW

Plan for tomorrow
start
living them today

We put off doing so many things and tell ourselves that the time is not right. When will the time be right? We are still face with the same choices and obstacles. Sometimes excuses seem more appropriate for us to remain in our comfort zone than reason for us to do those things required.

Many yesterdays have come and gone
waiting
for
tomorrow

ERROR

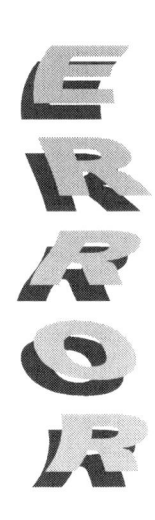

A
man that does not recognize his own error
is
a
man void of understanding

No one is above making mistakes because, we learn by
trial and error.

If we do no wrong, how do we justify, what is right?
We measure our growth by
error & awareness

Healing is Fighting for Yourself

Life is energy
and
to
live
is
a
daily challenge within our soul

Regardless
of
the darkness of our skies
daylight
surely returns and the sun is forever present

Therefore
heal with the Universe
and
let not circumstance or situation
cripple & paralyze
your
desire to live

TIME IS TRUTH

The moment we understand these two words
we
know life is forever

Mind
is
a
journey, traveling through time
accumulating & consolidating
experiences
to
give memory to the soul

LEARN TO LOVE YOURSELF

When
you learn to love you
someone else will have a reason too

EMOTIONS & GOOD SENSE

Learn to spend time with yourself and think. Thinking enhances your thoughts and gives you creativity. It allows you to be emotionally independent.

When a woman becomes sexually active, she becomes emotionally dependent, seeking a commitment from her partner, unless it is the understanding of the two that sex, is for the exchange of energy, without emotional attachment.

Men, are genders of seed therefore, lust is before love. Nevertheless, born of a woman, his quest for love is the same. He desires a woman who excites his fantasy and entertains his thoughts, just as she does. They are both looking for the same climax. He will find his way to you and you will be at the right place at the right time. You will find each other.

Too many people are with the wrong people for the wrong reasons. Be honest with yourself that you not cause anyone as well as yourself, unhappiness. Our choices & decisions are the paths we are destined to fulfill therefore, let yours be for the right reasons that happiness, find its way to you.

A Scholar in your own Right

Reason gives us
cause
&
effect

Once your footsteps
have
walked across the question marks
&
found the periods
you
are
now qualified to teach in exclamation

CHOICES & DESIRES

Sexual relationships without chemistry and understanding causes much conflict in one's life because, women are emotional and men are possessive. This is human nature.

Understand, without chemistry, there is not enough energy to draw the other. When time and energy becomes exhausted, know that it is time for change. It is time for self to re-examine its choices and do a self, examination: Am I happy? Why not and why am I surrendering myself to someone, who does not have my interest in his or her heart?

Life is of free will and our choices are to be of careful thought, your responsibility as well as mine. We must weigh the scale of justice & love before we say yes.

Happiness is about seeking our desires and reaching our goals. If I end up with you and you end up with me, how else can we not be together?

Corners & Dark Alleys

You
see things
you
never imagined to see
&
hear things
you
dare not repeat

FRAMES & FACES

Our emotions trigger our expressions and we change with
thought

Never under estimate, the power of truth
that
keeps us grounded and stabilized

We
can do anything we put our mind to
&
achieve our desired results through perseverance

Regardless
of
the emotions that frame our thoughts and paint our faces

FEEL IT!

We have to feel it to react to it
by
doing what is natural

Enjoying ourselves

Unrehearsed
not
a posted script

Because
life is an origin of itself

You
have to feel it!

SEXY

The sexiest people
are
people who are comfortable
with
themselves

Sexuality is the natural instinct of one's personifications.
We never know how we affect others
only
the way they affect us

We are always in the spotlight of someone's attention
as
we reverence truth
unconscious to the thought

Know
we are most admirable

Because
we are free within
&
we
allow others the same freedom
to
display
their naturalness

Action causes reaction
Now
that is sexy!

Today is as it Should Be

Many times our days are in question
because
it seems to have its own agenda
other
than the one planed

When
we do and have done all that we can do
giving
our best

Be
peaceful and recognize
today
as
a day as it is and was supposed to be

WHAT IS LIFE WITHOUT AN OPINION?

A
mind without thought

How
can we invent, build or progress
without
perception

Life
is
energy that gives us thought and imagination
from
this point, we form our own opinion

LOVE

Experience
the
energy of the sun that burns inside of our soul

The
earth in a cradle of water
is
an
open womb to the sun
transforming
energy into many forms of life
that
mate without question

Because
life is an experience
that
must be enjoyed through love

NOT A PERFECT SOUL

We
look for perfection in others
&
so easily, excuse the imperfection within ourselves

We
call our errors simple mistakes
&
everyone else

Crimes

STUBBORN

When
we
choose to ignore
wisdom & instruction
we
suffer the consequences
at
our own expense

Wisdom
&
common sense
has
A
lifetime of information
to
keep us or destroy us

Whom do we hurt being stubborn?

The See Saw

One end is up one end is down
&
when the minds are on one accord
both
ends
balance in the Universe

Understanding
is
the balance of opposites

Mama's Wisdom

My mother would always say to me
live your life today
as if you are going to court tomorrow

Always be able to justify your actions within the reasons
of truth. How can we grow in the light of understanding
if we refuse to accept the role of responsibility? The
manner in which we conduct ourselves is time
documented
the greatest feeling in the world is to know that you gave
your best in all of your efforts and endeavors, overcoming
your obstacles to achieve your goals. Whenever
our clock stops in this body, our thoughts carry on
&
we must be able to justify our actions with balance reasons.
All
of
this is to say
live your life in a manner
that
your reasons are in the light of truth
&
your name
becomes
a
memory of integrity & respect

Keep it Real the End Result is You

When
you choose to lie to yourself
you
disable
your factors to balance your scales
of
self worth

Like
still water filled with diseases

you are unable
to
heal or protect
the
most vital

You

DREAMS ARE MESSAGES WE LEARN TO UNDERSTAND

We dream in signs and symbols waiting for clarification
as we desperately try to interpret the meaning

Many times, we walk directly into the phase before we discover
this is the dream

The magnificent mind of the Creator
speaks to us
in our state of sub consciousness while we are between
the two Worlds

We learn that when we take our steps slowly in thought
with
an
honest heart
the
puzzle that is in bits and pieces
is
made known to us
in
measures
to
our level of understanding

EXPERIENCE IS THE BEST TEACHER

Because
these are the lessons we remember.

A
heart
of
understanding
will
be able to
see
the reasons for the endeavors

Because

explanation
is
the sigh of relief
we
welcome

I Got That Message

As
I was shopping one day
pushing
my cart through the store
a
woman approached me from behind
&
spoke
some vital information in my ear

She was straightforward in what she had to say

I
recognized the spirit of concern
in
her voice
and
appreciated her bravery in speaking out to me
I
needed that message
to
improve my situation.

She was a stranger without a face
&
had truth on her tongue

It was a rewarding day for me

When we listen and take heed to our messages
we
benefit to the highest effect

We Break Habits with Understanding

Just
because we're accustom
to
doing something repetitiously
Does Not
mean that we have no control to stop
We
create a comfort level of dependence
to
a particular thing & it becomes a habit

Some
habits are helpful
&
some are harmful
according to how they affect us

If
the habit benefit us
then
we have adopted a good thing
If
the nature of the habit projects harm
then
we suffer the consequences
From
our own weaknesses
as
a result

TRUTH TO HEART

Things people say
To & About
you

Instead
of
offense & defense
go
deep
within
check your truth section
to
see if there is any validity
to
the words spoken

If
you find any validity or truth
in
the words spoken
then
correct and polish you

Corrective criticism
many times is void of compassion
but
rich in truth
Stay true to yourself
Learn to Listen
with
an
open mind to better your self

Restrain Yourself

We must learn to know when to let go
to
let wisdom & peace execute their roles

When our positives makes us free from our negatives
we learn to make better choices
because
our
fears and inhibitions
no
longer have power over us

Open Your Eyes To The Truth

The
responsibility of truth is in our court
&
we must acknowledge
the
facts

If
we want better results
we
only have ourselves to blame
when
we
refuse to trust our instincts
to
open our eyes
to
what
is
staring us in the face

A Secret To Share

Someone to share a secret
with
is
your
oneness with trust

We entertain many loves in this life
but
all loves are not true loves

Then
you meet that one special person
who
confirms all of your beliefs

From
both sides of the coins
honesty
&
being young at heart
balances
the trust between two hearts
when
there is nothing to hide
you
share a secret

Your Purpose

Waking Up
to
yourself
is
the Greatest Gift
life
has to Offer

Elevate to the highest of your ability
with
Truth, Guts & Imagination

WITHOUT MAKE-UP

I
am
not talking
cosmetics

Be
the natural you

Your
thoughts your opinions
&
your mistakes

Your
smile and respect for life
is
the performance of a lifetime
We
Give & Receive so much from each other
when
we are free and natural
naked

Without
Make
Up

We all Have Bridges to Cross

Our lives consist of paths and destinations.
We arrive at these destinations by crossing our bridges.

There was a bridge in my hometown that would put me into a trance every time I saw it. I was eight years old & could not understand why I always experience these feeling looking at this bridge.

When I grew to be a young adult, I experienced a lot of disappointment & pain. My days felt pointless but I knew in all of my reality that as sure as there was a day & a night, my Creator would deliver me.
Then one day, years later when I got older and made a decision to do something about my tears I had a dream. I saw myself standing at the foot of that bridge with a made up mind. Then a headless entity came and ran me across that bridge,
I started jumping up & down in my happiness.

I
chose with the help of my higher power
to
cross that bridge

A Boat was Sent

One day, my daughter, another bystander and I were standing under a bus shelter waiting for a bus. When the bus arrived it was crowded and had standing room only. I had worked the night shift and did not feel like standing for the long ride home. I told my daughter that we would catch the next bus.

"Lo and behold," before the next bus arrived, we heard gunshots and looked up only to see two cars at a high speed coming toward us. I told my daughter and the other bystander to run in the opposite direction from me. I felt in my spirit that I would draw the cars to me.

As the cars got closer, a peace came over me before I blacked out. When I regain consciousness, I was lying peacefully in a bed of green grass and could not understand why. We all had been unconscious for a minute. Then I remembered my daughter was with me and we were in an accident. The paramedics had arrived placed us on stretchers & transported us to the hospital where we were treated for our bruises, hospitalized and released; we survived.

The point I am making is that the bus/boat came and I refused to board it and suffered the consequences whatever my excuse. I realized that sometimes in spite of how we may feel in our endeavors, we must press forward. The Boat came and I chose to stay in the comfort zone that caused me discomfort.

Our Goal and Our Dreams

Is
teaching our young
how
to
travel the Universe

Through
elevation and transformation
knowing
the
mind escapes the body
into
the mystery of the unknown

To
the seeker or believer
on
a
much higher plane

Than
the one of imagination

Read the Label

The label is the instruction

of

life
we constantly ignore
before
the tide rolls in to shore

Only
to
suffer the consequence
of
sorrow & regret

Victims of ourselves

Slow down
&
take the time to read the label

Young at Heart

Growing up is learning
&
exploring life

Young hearts are filled
with
the
magic of truth & imagination

As
we mature into the age of responsibility
circumstances
shed a dim light on our expectations
&
we lose faith
that
gives us the energy to focus
&
move forward

Our
magic becomes a foolish thought
&
we began to entertain doubt & fear
But
when
we embrace the most exciting times
in
our lives
we
laugh more than we cry

Let us stay
Young at Heart

Self to Blame

We
need to learn
to
take responsibility for our actions

Nobody
pushes our buttons

We
choose to let go

It is the consequence
that
brings us to reality

Who
can dispute the mechanisms of the universe
and
the wisdom of time
which
vibrates in the capsule of understanding

Therefore

"Know"
that
out of choice
we only have ourselves to blame

A Mother's Love

Is

An
Education

Because
she is our first teacher

A mother's love
Is
Protective

Within
her embrace we feel safe

A mother's love
will
endure until the end of time
because
our
internal cry is with her in mind

A Fool Will Lie to Himself

And
lose respect
in
the eyes of truth

21 at the age of 16

I
could not wait for twenty one
at
the age of sixteen

Ignoring
instruction & discipline
I
challenged wisdom

Surrounded
by
love
trying to preach my faults away

I refused to listen
to
the voice of patience
until
life
made me a student
of
the
greatest teachers of time

Pain
&
Disappointment

Both
gave me my certificate of understanding
16 is before 21

Messages

We
live by messages

Messages
save our lives
by
giving us warning
&
information
in
proper time

Be
careful
not
to
let
the lack of understanding
due
to
pride & stubbornness
keep you
from

receiving your messages
of
Truth & Wisdom

Signed,

A Message for You

ACKNOWLEDGMENTS

To
The Creator,

I thank you for all that you have done and do in my life.
Your wisdom is the height of my existence. I can only
share with others the greatest love I know
through all of my experiences and traumas, I look back
and see the messages you bestowed upon me.

Today, I realize that it was my blindness and
stubbornness
that
caused me to stumble and fall.
The messages were there, I remember them clearly now.
In your magnificence we are never without warning.
Today
I ask for consciousness with every breath to recognize
when
you are summoning me
To
Receive
My
Messages

ACKNOWLEDGEMENTS

To
All of my children

Sherron, Kennie, Danielle, and Terrelle and my beautiful goddaughter, Marnice, I thank you for being beautiful strong people. I look at each one of you and smile in my heart because I am thankful & grateful to have you in my life.

To all of my grandchildren & great grandchildren, Tom, Tiffany, Keeyonna, Lil Ken, Keenan, Dujuan, Drew, Terrez, Charrelle, Tyra and my great grandchildren Akila, Jamilla, Oria, Keena & Nicholas. I want you to know that you inspire me.

To my other daughters, the mothers of my grandchildren, Nancy and Renee, I applaud you for a good work in raising them to be loving and respectful people.

To my mom & dad who have passed on, I am ever grateful for you being my parents. You continue to be there for me at my lowest points of understanding. In my dreams, I acknowledge your presence of support reminding me of my spiritual strengths to endure and conquer my challenges. I love you and love is forever.

To my sisters Georgia and Eula, I adore you for being my sisters. Our relationship is so unique to me because you both have always been there with sisterly love & support. Tim and Kevin, you are the brothers I always wanted. I love you.

To my dearest friends I am truly grateful for the friendship we share & the candles we burned through our most challenging times. Penny, Samearl, Jean, Patrina, GiGi, (Stella & Bobby who have passed on), our laughter & tears made us stronger & walked us through those perilous times. To the many others that I have not mentioned, that I have met along the way; having played an important role in my life; I love you. You are deeply in my heart. I remember your truthfulness and kindness. The messages you gave me added to my growth.

I
thank you
all
who read and prosper from these messages

Ask
The Creator
for
the unimaginable blessings
in
your lives

A Message for You

Made in the USA
San Bernardino, CA
01 July 2016